Baby Steps

Mackenzie Wilson

BookLeaf Publishing

Baby Steps © 2023 Mackenzie Wilson

All rights reserved.

No part of this publication may be reproduced, stored in a retrieval system, or transmitted, in any form or by any means, electronic, mechanical, photocopying, recording or otherwise, without the prior written permission of the presenters.

Mackenzie Wilson asserts the moral right to be identified as author of this work.

Presentation by *BookLeaf Publishing*

Web: www.bookleafpub.com

E-mail: info@bookleafpub.com

ISBN: 9789357212625

First edition 2023

XX

Like all the women before me,
I've learned to carry burdens in the crook of my
hip
Balancing other's pain on top of my head,
Spread thin like wartime butter
I learned to say yes before I learned to say no
But like many girls
I was never taught my role explicitly
Instead, it seeps into you,
No matter how much you resist
From the sweat on your mother's brow
Your grandma's bad elbow
You hitch up your skirt,
And pick up where they left off

November

The November feeling that everything is too late
The warmth is gone
The sun has set
You can't go back to the way things were, or the
person you used to be
It's like missing a train you forgot you were
supposed to catch, and you don't remember till
you feel the icy gust of its wake
You're left there wondering how you could
possibly have done such a thing
How could you have forgotten to live while the
world was still alive?
Because now you must endure winter
And wait for spring to melt the earth, along with
your fingers and your toes and your heart

Faster

Fast
And narrowly
Weaving through traffic
We speed to arrive
Why do we always hurry?
Could we slow down a bit?
I'm scared that one day I'll realize
That I wasted my whole life rushing, then
Wish I hadn't reached the finish line so soon

Alive

Like trees growing on cliffsides
Flowers pressing through the cracks in concrete
Life is relentless
Unstoppable
It perseveres
That force lives inside us too
Whether we like it or not
We will march on
Leaning into the wind

Gardening

My mind was a garden of roses
Tangled and overgrown
They were the only flower I ever loved
The only I had known
But roses have one fatal flaw
Their sharp and spiky thorn
And what I thought was meant for me
Left me cut open, torn
I tried to trim the bushes
But to no avail
No matter what shears I used
I always seemed to fail
Then one day a seed flew in
On a breeze I didn't feel
It planted roots inside my head
I couldn't tell if it was real
But it began to bud and bloom
Into a soft, gentle horn
When I finally knelt to smell its scent
I was awakened, was reborn
The roses started to wilt
Decomposing into dirt
What was left was a flower
That would never leave me hurt
Now my brain is full of them

Beautiful, peaceful, pure
They saved me from the roses
A calla lily cure

Willful Negligence

We blind our eyes too easily
We feel the weight of our guilt in our fingertips
As we carry our garbage to the dumpster
But once the door is closed it's dismissed
Becoming someone else's problem
Somewhere else's problem
I don't think we should be allowed to forget so
easily
For the sake of those who won't get that liberty

Sunday

I want a lazy Sunday morning
One where we just sip coffee and watch tv,
maybe it's raining outside
We don't have to get up and pack our things
I just want to sit beside you on the couch and
rest my head on your shoulder and not think
about the fact that soon I'll have to say goodbye

Season's Greetings

Winter mandarins
Light blue air in your nostrils
A sky that's wet but feels so dry
Why does the coldest water always look the
most inviting?

Fangirl

She was a quiet kind of beautiful
Soft smile
Voice like honey
I don't know if the fire of her hair could melt the
ice behind her eyelids
But it certainly melted something in me

São Paulo

Terracotta buildings hidden in jungle green hills
Creeping up towards the sky
Slipping down into the mud
Murky brown water
Hands pressed against bus windows
Backs pressed to the door
20 million hopes and dreams crammed onto the
highway
Trees like umbrellas
Shading those below from the orange morning
light
Car horns in the distance
The São Paulo song

Tip-toe

12

I tip-toe across the creaky wooden floor so that I
don't make too much noise
I think to myself: a man would never do this
I keep tip-toeing

Father, Mother

Finding a lesson in everything
Adding to the conversation
Thumbs too large for iPhone buttons
Hairbrush through wet hair
Eating with guilt
Reaching for the milk

Measuring spoons
Opening your heart like the front door
Tidying for guests who never notice
Heading warnings you used to ignore
Emptying the dishwasher
Reading by the fire

'That Girl'

You don't need to be 'that'
You don't need to decide on an image of yourself
and spend your whole life trying to attain it
You can live every life you want to live
Without constantly rebranding yourself
You are not a brand
You are a girl
Not a fixed thing, not a commodity
You can take a new shape every day
Without declaring it to the world, or yourself
It doesn't matter if 'you're not that type of person'
Because you are that person
You are every person
You are everything
All at once

Calculated

15

Like a calculator, you know exactly which
buttons to press
All I can do is resist the push of your thumbs
And I am not my strongest in your hands
You keep making up new equations
I used to be dying to know the answer
Now I just want to be left alone

Crown Shyness

Like trees in the rainforest
Whose leaves never quite touch
We don't hug very often
But you hold me up

Favourites

I have a favourite everything
A favourite mug
A favourite spoon
A favourite song and place and view
But I never had a favourite person
Not until you

Selflessness

Wherever you are, I hope the sun is shining
And you woke up excited for the day
I hope you've laughed already
Maybe a couple of times even
It's cloudy here, and no one's around to tell me
any jokes
But I still only find myself wishing
That you're happier than me

At least I still have the sunset

Even if I am alone
At least I still have the sunset
The clouds in the sky
There are probably birds chirping somewhere
And if I walked
I'm sure I could find some waves hitting a shore
I might be alone
But the world is still turning its usual turn
If nothing else
The sun will set
The sun will rise
My lungs will continue to expand and contract
with each breath
And it will be okay

One by one

I'd pluck out my eyelashes,
One by one,
If I knew every wish would come true
I'd pluck out my eyelashes,
One by one,
And use every wish on you

Confirmation Bias

I wonder what it's like to have the self-assurance
of some men
To think of yourself first
To never get tired of your own voice
I wonder what it's like to be unaware of your
biases
Finding confirmation of long-held beliefs
everywhere you go
It's very easy to see the world how you want to
Unless you are marginalized and wish to see it
as fair

Happy to be sad

I mourn every conversation we haven't gotten to
have
Every late-night talk
And morning kiss
Every movie that we've said we'll watch but
haven't found the time for
I know that it's better to love you from a
distance than not love you at all,
But if there's a galaxy out there where the two of
us weren't separated by space, by time,
Where we lived in the same city
And walked home from school together
Where you came over if I needed you, and held
me until everything was alright
Then I would rather be there
Please don't take offense
Because already, regardless
I am the luckiest girl in the world
But I can't say I would mind being the luckiest
girl in the universe